101 BUSINESS LEADERSHIP "TIPS" TO LIVE BY

101 BUSINESS LEADERSHIP "TIPS" TO LIVE BY

A PRACTICAL GUIDE TO GETTING THE MOST FROM YOUR TEAM, YOUR BUSINESS, AND YOURSELF!

STEVE POPKIN, MBA
RANDALL MICHEL, MD FACS

PALMETTO
PUBLISHING
Charleston, SC
www.PalmettoPublishing.com

© 2024 Steve Popkin, MBA
Randall Michel, MD FACS
All rights reserved.
No portion of this book may be reproduced,
stored in a retrieval system, or transmitted in
any form by any means–electronic, mechanical,
photocopy, recording, or other–except for
brief quotations in printed reviews,
without prior permission of the author.

Paperback ISBN: 979-8-8822-5952-1

INTRODUCTION

If you are leading a business, you undoubtedly have the requisite industry skills and knowledge. However, what will determine the level of your personal success and that of your business is the way you interact with your employees and others; how you develop and execute your strategic and operational plans; how you go about making the best possible decisions; how you communicate internally and externally; how you keep yourself organized and on-point; how you optimize your leadership team and how you build company-wide engagement, productivity, and esprit de corps.

It may seem that accomplishing these fundamental steps to success just takes common sense or is inherent in business leaders. To a great degree it is just common sense. Most business leaders know what they should be doing to optimally lead their company and maximize their personal success, but many business leaders don't do it...or at least not to the degree they *know* they should. Why is that? The answer is simple...*it's hard!* Business leaders have the constant battle of determining and communicating priorities, weighing critical decisions, and dealing with the positive and potentially negative consequences of those decisions. When in the situational pressure-cooker, business leaders sometimes abandon, even if just briefly, the tangential leadership qualities and actions that, in aggregate, are critical to the success of their company, as well as their own personal success and reputation. *101 Business Leadership "Tips" to Live By* is not intended to teach you how to do anything (well maybe a few things), but rather to constantly poke you in the ribs and remind you of what you know you should be doing and encourage you to do it.

Read this book all the way through, it will take you less than an hour. Then keep it on your desk (or in your drawer if you're embarrassed!) and flip through it again every week or two. After a while, the "tips" will be embedded in your mind and will become your natural way of leading. At that point, just refer back to the book every couple of months for a shot of encouragement.

Dr. Randall Michel and I are very pleased to pass on these business leadership "tips" acquired through *many* years of leading hospitals and healthcare organizations from our Chief Medical Officer and Chief Executive Officer positions, respectfully. We would be thrilled if *101 Business Leadership "Tips" to Live By* was of assistance to you in reaching your personal and business goals.

--Steve Popkin

Always act through the lens of optimizing...

- ✓ Staff Engagement-Productivity-Morale
- ✓ Sound Decision-Making
- ✓ Team Development
- ✓ Reputation
- ✓ Communication
- ✓ Execution
- ✓ Organization
- ✓ Strategic Thinking
- ✓ Innovation
- ✓ Leadership
- ✓ Operational Efficiency
- ✓ Financial Stewardship

1.

When you have sufficient information to make a decision, pull the trigger

2.

What you decide **_not to do_** can be just as important as what you decide **_to do_**

3.

Give up some upside gain to limit downside risk

4.

Win-lose is okay for single transactions, but win-win is needed for sustainable operations and relationships

5.

There are rules and policies for a reason, but you can override them if the situation necessitates

6.

In this increasingly fast-changing environment, think 40% short term, 40% medium term and 20% long-term

7.

Keep asking your team questions until you are satisfied that you have sufficient and accurate information--this tends to improve the quality of input going forward

8.

Encourage dissenting opinions--it will make for better final decisions

9.

Do the math--make sure what sounds good in concept pencils out

10.

Trust but verify regarding information and accounts of situations

11.

Spend on small things that have big impact on how people feel, but evaluate and negotiate the big expense items

12.

Sometimes you need to serve in the role of mediator/arbitrator

13.

Give your direct reports regular performance feedback--their annual evaluation should not be a surprise

14.

Have regular (i.e., weekly) meetings with your leadership team as a group

15.

Send relevant articles to your leadership team. It will let them know what you feel is important or interesting, and will show interest in their development.

16.

Give your leaders
important projects
and let them fly

17.

If you disagree with a team member, express it respectfully and thank them for their opinion

18.

Try to foster an us against the world mentality

19.

When you have formed positive personal and professional relationships, holding staff accountable is easier and more impactful

20.

Getting involved with external organizations can bring great benefit to you and your organization

21.

Prepare, prepare, prepare--it reduces your stress and enhances peoples' perception of you

22.

Follow-through on *everything*

23.

Track, gather
and publish your
team's/organization's
accomplishments
each year

24.

Be the face of
the organization,
but let others
have their turns

25.

Don't take yourself
(and some situations)
too seriously

26.

Make efforts to, and develop techniques to, remember peoples' names

27.

Be visible and approachable

28.

It's nice to be liked, but more important to have earned respect

29.

Get to know your employees as much as possible, without becoming too personal

30.

Address issues brought forth by individuals *as soon as possible*

31.

You don't have
to be the smartest
person in the room

32.

Give credit to others; let your team members shine

33.

Remember that your words and comments have oversized impact. Your colleagues may not always perceive your words and comments as you intended.

34.

Keep your leadership
team and others
in the know to the
degree possible

35.

Maintain the proverbial open-door policy. Explain to your management staff why allowing employees to break the chain of command is okay.

36.

Don't avoid public speaking,
even if you hate it

37.

Communicate
often and broadly

38.

Develop and execute an external communication plan

39.

As much as possible, listen to the comments and opinions of others before expressing yours

40.

If you receive compliments about employees, email them out to all employees--it builds esprit de corps

41.

Send personal notes of praise and/or gratitude to employees and other constituents

42.

Hardwire processes --don't rely on each employee doing the right thing every time

43.

Don't micro-manage, but micro-monitor. Make sure what is supposed to be getting done is getting done.

44.

Embrace needed change and innovation--don't let your industry pass you by

45.

Meet with the staff of each department by yourself to receive candid input.
Then act on the input quickly, where appropriate.

46.

Each morning organize your day and prepare a daily to do list in your journal, which becomes your "bible"

47.

Throughout the day or after, enter things in your journal that need to be addressed or remembered

48.

If something makes it to your journal list, make sure it gets done, and done quickly

49.

If something doesn't get crossed off your journal list that day, carry it forward to the next day, but don't let it get stale

50.

Prepare a quarterly(ish) master project list in your journal. Taking it out of your head and putting it on paper will keep you organized and reduce your stress.

51.

Get a great Executive Assistant and let her or him keep things humming

52.

Keep the plates spinning--don't let anything crash and break

53.

You're the conductor of the orchestra. You don't have to be the virtuoso, but you have to make sure the virtuoso is playing the music the way you intend.

54.

Know what's going on in "your house"

55.

Retain final say on decisions regarding serious disciplines or terminations

56.

Hire for attitude

57.

Think of career paths for your stars and don't forget succession planning

58.

Treat younger staff like you would want employers to treat your employed children or treat you when you were younger

59.

Have employment and compensation policies that are fair to all

60.

Have a team member or committee focus on morale building activities, and have senior management lead the events

61.

Have employee contests (i.e., cost savings, revenue growth, etc.).
In addition to generating good business ideas, it enhances employee engagement.

62.

Have a place where employees can post personal things
(i.e., pet adoption, band for hire, etc.)

63.

Don't hire in
your likeness;
hire to fill the gaps

64.

Check your ego
at the door;
you can pick it up
on the way out

65.

Budget and prepare for unexpected occurrences

66.

Do things to help people when you can; it will help you when you can't

67.

When on a virtual meeting, pay attention, don't multi-task

68.

Except in social situations, don't ask questions for which you will not make use of the answers

69.

Remove macro and micro barriers to efficiency. It will help with productivity, employee satisfaction and staff turnover.

70.

Balance risk taking and risk avoidance. Know when to use or conserve cash.

71.

Know how to listen. When you ask a question be prepared to listen to the answer. Listening is being willing to be informed by another person.

72.

Have a good idea of what you wish to accomplish before calling a meeting

73.

Protect your integrity; your reputation is your most valuable asset

74.

Try never to make another feel ignorant or stupid. This is something a person rarely forgets or forgives.

75.

Learn to look at situations and problems from multiple angles. Try to anticipate unintended consequences of your decisions.

76.

Gain some understanding of your personal biases

77.

Try to eliminate emotion from your decision process whenever possible

78.

Kicking the can down the road isn't always a bad thing

79.

Give credit and recognition to your staff, but avoid overdoing it to the point that it becomes meaningless. Praise in public, criticize or coach in private.

80.

Appropriate use of
humor can be
a valuable tool
(if it comes naturally)

81.

Try to recognize when you have made a mistake and own it. As once said, "good judgment comes from experience, and a lot of that comes from bad judgment."

82.

Define or avoid use of acronyms unless you are sure your "audience" knows their meaning

83.

Establish a balance
in meetings between
efficiency and
allowing voices
to be heard

84.

Don't ask a question when you are certain of the answer, unless it is a teaching situation

85.

If you know someone in your organization is not working out after opportunities for improvement, make a change sooner rather than later

86.

Always be ready
to learn something
new every day

87.

Calm demeanor and consistency can be reassuring to staff

88.

Try to avoid using 20 or more words to say yes or no

89.

Break down processes into component parts, then build them back better

90.

When confronted with complex problems remember the axiom:
"The simplest explanation is usually the best one"

91.

Be circumspect in dealing with those who profess to know all the answers

92.

Seek advice from trusted sources and give such input careful consideration, realizing you are ultimately responsible for your decisions

93.

Encourage your team to bring you potential solutions when they bring you problems

94.

If a proposal is good today, it should be good tomorrow--few decisions require an emergency response

95.

Try to never lose sight of the big picture; in which direction are you trying to steer the ship?

96.

As in chess, try to think several moves ahead

97.

If something seems too complex for someone to explain, question the understanding of the person doing the explaining

98.

Separate facts from opinions, and give each their appropriate weight

99.

Be aware of existential threats to your organization's success

100.

"Because that's the way we've always done it" is not a good answer

101.

Proof your emails for content, spelling and grammar. Double check the recipients. Be extra careful about tone, as the recipient has no context other than your words.

NOTES

www.ingramcontent.com/pod-product-compliance
Lightning Source LLC
LaVergne TN
LVHW051953060526
838201LV00059B/3626